DIAMONDS

Text and Photographs
Fred Ward

Editing
Charlotte Ward

Carat for carat, fine diamonds are among the most desirable and expensive items on earth. Perhaps the world's most famous and storied gem, the 45.52-carat fancy deep greyish blue Hope Diamond came to Washington's Smithsonian Institution in 1959 as a gift to the American people from legendary New York dealer Harry Winston. Now it is the museum's most visited object on display.

HISTORY
AND LORE

T HE DIAMOND MYSTIQUE. The long history, the storied romances, the intrigues, even the murders. What primal magic sets one gemstone apart from all others? What unique allure graces this best known and most coveted of all jewels? Is it the name itself? Say the word, *Diamonds*, and the mind fills with dazzling images of shimmering facets, potentates, great wealth, glamorous women, and the style and taste to own and wear the best. *Diamonds*. The standard of price, beauty, and value against which all other gems are measured. *Diamonds*. The incomparable gem.

Diamonds are more than unsurpassed beauty and sparkle. In no other gemstones are so many desirable attributes combined. Diamonds are the hardest material on earth, and, as far as we know, in the universe. When Friedrich Mohs devised his 1 to 10 hardness scale, he set diamonds at 10 and worked down from that point. Hardness alone would still make diamonds indispensable as an industrial tool if not as a gem.

Indians had already enjoyed an illustrious millennia-long legacy of gem appreciation when they discovered diamonds about 800 B.C. The honor for the earliest gems collected most likely belongs not to diamonds but to pearls, harvested ready for use, exquisitely finished by nature. No one can say when the first person picked up and kept the first specimen of any gemstone. But we can identify periods when people began regularly mining and wearing different gems. Workers dug into Upper Egypt's desert hills, at what later became known as Cleopatra's Mines, to extract emeralds as early as 2000 B.C.

The discovery of diamonds in rich alluvial deposits around Golconda, India, changed the history of gems forever. Although miners never located the volcanic source, sufficient quantities came from nearby river beds and flats to provide the world with most of its diamonds until the 1700s. No matter that many larger mines would later be found in other countries. Out of India's gravel and sand came some of the world's best and most famous diamonds, each evolving a lore all its own.

A fabled and well-documented history surrounds the naturally-colored **Dresden Green Diamond.** *Taken to London around 1726, the 41-carat Indian gem sold to Saxony's ruler in 1741. First incorporated into the* **Order of the Golden Fleece,** *it was later worked into this hat ornament.*
Courtesy The Green Vaults, Dresden, Germany

Diamonds were found as early as 800 B.C. near Golconda, India, where mining continued until the 1700s. Old drawings (left) show miners working some of the alluvial deposits in caves. Despite primitive conditions, the area produced some of the greatest diamonds ever uncovered, including the Smithsonian's twin blues, the **Blue Heart** *(above) and* **Hope** *(cover), as well as the spectacular table-cut* **Dari-i-nur** *(opposite, far right). Other Indian diamonds, as in the necklace and trays (opposite), fill cases in the fabulous Crown Jewels of Iran display in Tehran.*

Desire for the *Hope, Blue Heart, Dari-i-nur,* and the infamous *Koh-i-noor,* now in England's Queen Mother's Crown, have shaped history. Often with famed and named diamonds, royal involvement brought dramatic events. To safeguard the *Koh-i-noor,* 19th-century Afghan prince Shah Shuja endured blinding and days of torture. Finally surrendering his prize, he incongruously explained his defiant stand, "It brings good luck."

L uck is but one in a seemingly endless list of powers early owners attributed to diamonds. Health and financial claims permeate diamond lore. Diamonds were said to cure insanity and impotence while protecting against the effects of plague, pestilence, and poisons. For proof Indians pointed out that the plague first attacked poor people, who had no

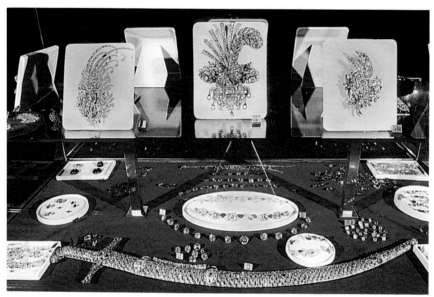

diamonds. Maharajahs, shahs, and sultans staked lives and empires to possess the biggest and best, often looting each others' treasuries. For centuries rulers accumulated all available jewels. Diamonds remain the visible symbols of authority and privilege.

As Indian supplies dwindled, Brazil discovered diamonds in 1725 to become the world's principal source until South Africa's massive deposits rewrote diamond history. Beginning in 1866 when someone noticed a child playing with a shiny "toy" that turned out to be a diamond, the entire development of southern Africa altered to accommodate the influx of people and money from the ensuing rush. Geologists learned that diamonds reached the earth's surface via volcanic vents, or "pipes," and the chase was on to find these rich primary sources. Chaos and frantic mining on 31 foot square claims

THE RHODES COLOSSUS
STRIDING FROM CAPE TOWN TO CAIRO.

Everything about the diamond business changed in the 1860s with huge South African discoveries. Once he consolidated four chaotic Kimberley diamond mines into the syndicate that would become De Beers, Cecil Rhodes (left) spread his influence across Africa. One result has been a steady supply of quality diamonds, such as the D-flawless gem (above), at mainly stable prices.

At Kimberley's Big Hole thousands of miners dug on claims each 31 feet square. Free enterprise defeated efficiency. Deadly cave-ins were frequent. With the largest check written until then (worth about $200 million today), Cecil Rhodes bought control of the mine. A lake that formed at the bottom of the pit after the mine closed in 1914 is now over 500 feet deep.

produced two undesirable results: an uncontrolled market and inefficient gem recovery. As individuals dumped huge amounts of diamonds into the market, prices plummeted, making it less profitable to mine. In fact, during such occasional gluts, miners actually left milk cans packed with diamonds unattended at the train station, to be transported to town without guards.

Enter two of the most extravagant characters in gem history, Cecil Rhodes and Barney Barnato. Both saw a need and conceived a solution. The dream of both men was to organize and consolidate diamond mining. Only one could be the winner. Each bought every available Kimberley Mine share until finally in 1888 Rhodes outmaneuvered Barnato in a deal that still affects every diamond sold in the world. With the largest check written until then, £5,338,650 (worth more than $200 million today), Rhodes created De Beers Consolidated Mines, Ltd. (named for two brothers whose farm held two diamond mines). Since the 1920s De Beers has controlled and marketed diamonds as no other gemstone has ever been controlled and marketed.

*In addition to the **Hope**, Washington's Smithsonian Institution is home to a dazzling variety of famous diamonds. A modern necklace with smaller stones lies inside the **Napoleon Necklace**, with its large diamond drops. Marie Antoinette wore the accompanying earrings on the left.*

Individual gems include a 28.30-carat marquise-cut ring (upper left) and center trio; the 18.30-carat yellow Shephard; *the 16.70-carat round* Pearson; *and the eerily fluorescing 127-carat* Portuguese. *The Blue Heart (top right) and the 67.90-carat brownish* Victoria Transvaal *are sumptuous fancies.*

R hodes went on to more exploits, established a world famous scholarship fund, and even had a country named for him—Rhodesia. After a period of reorganization, De Beers began to prosper under the inspired and tough leadership of Ernest Oppenheimer, who forced his way onto the board, becoming chairman in 1929, and began setting De Beers policy that continues to this day.

Observing that diamond prices could only be stable if he managed supplies, Oppenheimer contracted to buy the entire annual outputs of countries and mines. With inventory far exceeding aristocratic consumption, De Beers mounted a mainly U.S. campaign promoting a diamond for every bride. Oppenheimer's plan, implemented by him throughout his long life and then by son Harry until his recent retirement, was as unique as the gem he traded. Not only does De Beers annually mine over half the world's gem diamonds (by value) but it also markets about 70 percent of all uncut diamonds. Of its $200 million advertising budget, De Beers spends more than half on U.S. promotions alone. With the stability produced by De Beers's purchases, financing, and marketing, diamond prospecting proceeded for decades at an unprecedented pace. Mining activity spread from South Africa to Namibia, Zaire, Angola, Sierra Leone, Ghana, Tanzania, Guinea, Central African Republic, Ivory Coast, Liberia, and Botswana.

Discoveries in the Siberian permafrost half a century ago rocked the system. Because of the quantity and quality of its gems, the then-Soviet Union made early attempts to circumvent De Beers. The old government

For more than 2000 years, monarchs reserved diamonds for themselves. The entire concept of gem ownership changed dramatically in the 1800s and early 1900s with the rise of democracy, salaries for pay, and the huge diamond discoveries in Africa, where this 253.7-carat octahedron originated. Royalty became less common, and massive numbers of gems needed homes. Global marketing targeted diamonds for engagements, anniversaries, and other special occasions. For the first time in history, diamonds were forever, and for everyone.

Oppenheimer Diamond by Chip Clark, Smithsonian Institution

finally realized it could generate more hard currency within the system, so De Beers marketed most of Siberia's output for years. Since the Soviet Union breakup, Russia has continued selling most of its uncut gem diamonds through De Beers, although the two operate under an increasingly strained relationship. Contract signings are routinely delayed and agreement lengths shortened. Russia regularly insists on selling more and better-grade diamonds outside the De Beers system, and does, with or without agreements.

What's in a name? A flashy profit. Brown diamonds used to be considered industrials until Australia's Argyle Mine taught the trade a lesson by renaming them "cognac" and "champagne" and promoting them as gems. Whereas every diamond mine produces an occasional colored stone, Argyle bases its reputation on color. Although only one in 90,000 of its diamonds is pink, enough are available for matched pink masterpieces (pages 40-41). Opening in 1986, Argyle already mines more than 42 million carats annually, the world's largest volume.

Today's diamond rushes proceed almost unnoticed in Canada's frozen West and in Colorado. More than 50 million acres in Alberta, Saskatchewan, and the Northwest Territories have been claimed or staked for diamond exploration. All indicators suggest large reserves both in primary kimberlite pipes, as well as in glacial deposits. The Kelsey Lake, Colorado mine, North America's only commercial diamond mine, has produced more than 20,000 carats, including a 28.3-carat yellow and 14.2-carat white.

Potential diamond buyers ask if the world will run out of diamonds or if some new find will collapse prices. Neither seems likely. Since our planet's infancy, diamonds have formed and are still forming today a hundred miles beneath our feet. But those new diamonds are unlikely to be exposed on the earth's surface for millions of years. Will there be more large, important diamond finds? Of course. Our planet holds many more gem surprises.

THE HUNT FOR
TREASURE

In many cases diamond's properties far exceed the nearest pretender. It is the hardest material–it cannot be scratched. Its molar density, the number of atoms per unit volume, is greater than all other forms of matter. Its thermal conductivity is five times better than copper's. It has the lowest compressibility of all known materials. Its gage factor...five times greater than silicon's. It is not degraded at temperatures that would make silicon wilt. It even emits electrons in a vacuum and may be the basis for future flat panel displays. Diamond is the ultimate material.

C. Jim Russell, *Diamond Depositions*

Unlike rubies, sapphires, and emeralds, which are chemical compounds, diamonds are the crystalline form of a single element, carbon. So is graphite, the black lubricant and the "lead" in pencils. Graphite and diamonds are different forms of carbon—one is common and inexpensive, the other among the most valuable materials on earth.

To transform carbon into natural diamonds requires two things—heat and pressure. When pressures exceed 580,000 pounds per square inch and temperatures soar above 1000°C, carbon can crystallize into diamond. This precise condition naturally exists at only one place. Diamonds form in molten rock well below the earth's surface in a relatively thin band between 75 and 120 miles underground, within the asthenosphere.

Most gems crystallize at a wide variety of depths beneath the earth's surface. In order for people to find them, they must rise through or almost through the earth's crust, usually by the mountain-building process, which slowly lifts rocks, dirt, and gems. Over vast periods of time the dirt overburden erodes, leaving gems relatively concentrated and close at hand. At our current level of rather primitive mining development, if gems do not end up in the top 2000 feet—the thin skin of earth's crust—we will probably never find them.

Consolidated Diamond Mines, on Namibia's Atlantic coast, is one of the few De Beers operations where workers can come into direct contact with gems. After huge earthmoving equipment removes up to 80 feet of sand, miners sweep the bedrock clean looking for precious diamond crystals.

New and old mines together assure a steady flow of diamonds. Botswana had no mines until 1967, when De Beers geologists traced three crystals to their source. Afternoon blasts (above, left) still shattered the surface at Orapa in 1978. Now the small undeveloped country is the world's largest producer of gem diamonds. Today the mile-wide crater at Orapa's Jwaneng Mine is already several hundred feet deep. Tunnel drillers at South Africa's Premier Mine (below) work 2,000 feet below ground in an old mine that in 1905 produced the largest diamond ever found, the 3,106-carat Cullinan.

In the mid-1800s, Brazil was the world's largest diamond supplier. Although Brazil continues mining diamonds, its heyday was between the demise of India's deposits and the great discoveries in South Africa.

In the molten ooze where they crystallize, diamonds have a precarious birth. Whereas other gems often form in the host rocks where they are found, diamonds require a singular route to discovery. They must be blasted to the earth's surface in a volcanic eruption. If convection currents swirl them deeper into the magma, they revert to free carbon atoms. If they cool slowly as they rise, they transform to graphite. If they contact oxygen while they are still hot, they vaporize into carbon dioxide. Only if they blast from the upper mantle to the earth's surface and cool rapidly do they survive as diamonds. Even then, De Beers estimates it has to move 250 tons of material for every finished diamond carat. The earth does not give up its riches lightly.

Kimberlite, a conglomerate rock named for Kimberley, South Africa, where it was first identified, carries almost all diamonds upward. An exception, lamproite, is the transporting rock in Australia. Although about 450 volcanoes have erupted a total of 2,500 times in recorded history, few have kimberlite, and only one in a hundred kimberlite pipes is a profitable diamond producer—only two dozen or so in the world. In Canada's present diamond rush, prospectors are following kimberlite trails toward volcanic pipes, which, if they are lucky, will finally become diamond mines.

Kimberlite pipes are known as primary diamond deposits. They vary from a few hundred feet across, in Arkansas, to more than a mile wide in Orapa, Botswana. The pipe is so big that even though miners work around the clock, they only lower the open pit about a foot a year. Once located and test drilled, productive pipes can be mined for many decades. For example, the Premier Mine in South Africa, which yielded the world record 3,106-carat *Cullinan* in 1905, is still producing. Russia's large mine at Mir and Australia's Argyle are both primary deposits.

Diamonds apparently form under continents beneath the relatively

Over hundreds of millions of years diamonds washed down from South Africa's highland volcanic pipes to the Namibian coast. Consolidated Diamond Mine gathers gems from the beach while Debmarine uses ships to pump gravel from the offshore ocean bottom, separating the diamonds while still at sea (above).

large, stable cooler plates, or shields, called "cratons." Prospectors discover most diamond mines within areas lying on top of great cratons—southern and western Africa, eastern South America, Siberia, and Australia. One of the largest such cratons exists under Canada.

Secondary diamond deposits are alluvial, found not where gems surfaced but where they washed to a new location. India, Brazil, Venezuela, and most of west Africa have alluvial deposits. Whether volcanic eruptions built diamond-bearing mountains or entire areas were lifted during mountain building, the results were the same. Over time, wind and water slowly leveled the hills, exposing diamonds. Water or glacial action pushed the diamonds to new sites, often hundreds or thousands of miles from their birth pipes.

South of Namibia's "Skeleton Coast" the world's most unusual diamond mine is not a mine in any traditional sense, yet it produces the highest percentage of gem diamonds anywhere. Consolidated Diamond Mine (CDM) has no kimberlite pipe, no alluvial river flats, and no fixed deposit. The "mine" is a strip of beach more than 100 miles long. The diamonds in this rich area reached the surface half a country away, via South African volcanoes. Over an almost inconceivable time as the volcanoes eroded flat, diamonds, dirt, and gravel debris washed down rivers toward the Atlantic Ocean. Some of the heavier diamonds sank into the ocean floor while others were pushed to the beach by storms and sea currents. It is likely only a material as hard as diamonds could have survived such an arduous trip.

Separating what is often far less than a carat of diamonds per ton of rocks is a costly and tedious process. The traditional separator was a slanted table coated with grease (upper left). Diamonds stick to grease while a slurry of gravel floats by. To avoid worker temptation, the mines instituted elaborate schemes with gloves inside sealed glass boxes. The latest automatic separator relies on diamonds fluorescing under high intensity x-rays. Delicate sensors detect the minute glow, triggering an instantaneous blast of air (above) that blows the gem (and a few pieces of gravel) out of a stream of fast-moving ore.

Russia inherited from the USSR a large diamond stockpile it wants to sell and a De Beers contract it wants to alter. Years of negotiations are likely. Siberia's mines, such as snow-rimmed Aikhal, produce high quality crystals. A harsh climate with 100 foot permafrost makes mining difficult.

A diamond mine can be profitable with 5 percent gems and 95 percent near-gems and industrials. CDM reverses all norms, producing up to 95 percent gem diamonds, about a million carats a year onshore and off-shore from Debmarine. The reason for the percentage is obvious. Only higher quality, tough gem diamonds could have survived the trip to the beach that may have taken hundreds of millions of years.

For decades onshore mining at CDM was basically a sand moving operation. After carefully selecting a new area, gigantic vehicles removed the sand overburden, up to 80 feet deep. Workers then swarmed over the exposed bedrock where the heavier diamonds had sunk over time. Using small shovels and brushes, employees scoured every crevice, picking up loose diamonds by hand. To avoid the obvious security issues of ingestion and frequent searches, CDM signed on workers for 6-month shifts within compounds surrounded by miles of guarded fences. This policy reduced searches to only 2 a year. Now CDM removes most beach sand, builds dams around search areas, floods them with several feet of water, then vacuums water, sand, and diamonds. Machine-separation of diamonds cuts the security risk.

As the hunt for diamonds broadens, De Beers continues to be a major prospecting force. But individual firms and countries also seek new deposits. Profiting from the experience in South Africa after the great Kimberley find, prospectors realized that the obvious first place to look for a new diamond mine is near an old one. Whatever conditions made one

Argyle's Amazing Pink
and Red Diamonds

Australia's Argyle Mine (top) sprang onto the scene almost fully grown, producing 29 million carats in its first year, 1986. Since then it has increased output to more than 42 million carats, a third of the world's supply but only 6 to 7 percent of its value, because most of its stones are small and off-color (above, right). However, its fame rests on more than size or volume. Before Argyle, few mines produced pink or red diamonds. Argyle is famous both for its number of pinks and as the sole source of intense pinks (opposite). Buyer interest soared when a 3.14-carat pink Argyle gem sold at auction for $1.65 million. Argyle reversed the market's view of colored diamonds with a successful global campaign to sell its various shades of brown as "champagne" and "cognac." Argyle has developed robots for cutting many of its better quality gems (above, left).

"Fancies" flaunt their rainbow colors. Diamonds are far more than colorless gems. Even at premium prices, fancy colored diamonds in almost every hue attract devoted collectors.

A De Beers's collection of unfaceted fancy colored diamonds is on private display in London. Small amounts of trace elements, such as boron for blue and nitrogen for yellow, are responsible for the color in diamonds.

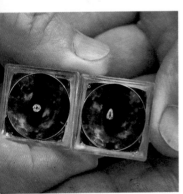

America's own diamond mine is the Crater of Diamonds State Park in Arkansas. For a small fee, tourists dig all day and keep what they find. Not many visitors proceed with the vigor of James Archer (top), who has dug practically every day for 18 years. One or two diamonds a day turn up in the park, usually small industrials (above). But the lure of buried treasure is enough to bring diggers back for more. Occasionally police officers adopt the habits of the people they watch by sporting gold and diamond badges.

Tony Perrn Collection

Among the largest and nicest Arkansas diamonds in private hands is the unfaceted 4.25-carat yellow Kahn Diamond, found in 1977. Hillary Clinton wore the stone set in a necklace for the governor's 1979 inauguration. She wore it reset as a ring at President Clinton's 1993 Inaugural Ball.

Kahn Jewelry

explosive volcanic eruption deliver diamonds to the surface may well have caused others nearby. That happy circumstance seems to be the rule. Once De Beers located the first diamond deposit in Botswana, it soon found others within the country. In the last decade Russians have uncovered at least two more Siberian diamond deposits, and the Australians recently located another deposit near Argyle.

Antarctica is the only vast land area with all the right geology but thus far no diamonds. Since several cratons have been identified, its future as a reserve seems promising. However, international agreements prohibit mining the frozen continent.

Despite popular misconceptions about sources, more than 90 percent of new diamonds come from only 5 countries: Australia-42 millions of carats a year; Zaire-21.9; Botswana-17.7; Russia-12.5; and South Africa-10.2. The lineup differs when countries are tallied by the value of their diamonds: Russia leads with diamonds worth about $2 billion annually; Botswana follows, then South Africa, Australia, and Zaire. The global production of diamonds is estimated at $6.5 billion to $7.2 billion. There are more diamonds mined and marketed now than at any other time in history. Fortunately for De Beers, the producing countries, and the gem trade, more people than ever are buying diamonds.

When touring museums or viewing antique jewelry auctions, you might think from viewing the number of gems in ornate jewelry that diamonds used to be plentiful. However, estimates from old mines and production figures from today suggest the rarity of old finds and the success of recent diamond prospecting and mining. Of the two and a quarter billion carats (450 metric tons) ever mined, 22 percent came in one recent 5-year period. Between 1986 and 1990, Argyle's first years of operation, the single Australian deposit produced 8 percent of all the diamonds ever mined in history. More than 80 percent of uncut, or rough, diamonds are industrials and near-gems, not the stuff of dreams. Even with such production numbers, fine finished gem diamonds continue to be extraordinarily rare.

25

ROMANCING
THE STONE

Diamonds are nature's most perfect creation. Their structure, hardness, brilliance, and beauty are unsurpassed. The epitome of desire, diamonds are frozen pieces of time, gifts from the planet's interior, eternal links with nature. And yet, as ideal as the gems' qualities are, few owners would wear the crystals as they come from the ground. To make them gorgeous requires a little inspired human intervention.

Capturing the prismatic wonder of rainbows, faceted diamonds cast their spell by reflecting light from dozens of minute mirrored surfaces. The combination of precise facets and diamond's extraordinarily high refractive index create a paradoxical firelike movement in the depths of what is a solid lifeless gem crystal. Indian craftsmen cut and polished colored gems long before diamond's discovery. But, there is a vast difference between fashioning a softer colored stone into a dome, called a cabochon, and cutting and polishing tiny facets on the hardest material on earth.

No records exist concerning the first attempts to cut, fashion, facet, and polish diamonds; but unquestionably those efforts occurred in India. Some surviving examples, such as the *Dari-i-nur* (see page 5), show that early lapidaries had little comprehension of refraction or the benefits of faceting. However, they obviously mastered polishing and bruting, using one diamond as a tool to shape another.

Since Indian and Persian rulers apparently admired uncut colored gem crystals, one unanswered question is why so few rough Indian diamonds survive. Did the wealthy not find diamond crystals appealing, or were the old roughs later cut once faceting became popular? Renaissance Europeans blended art and science to refine gem technology. Faceting skills spread around the world. No one knows how many great old uncut or poorly cut gems were initially faceted or refaceted between 1400 and 1900.

Lapidaries over the centuries revised designs and later applied mathematics in search of the perfect diamond shape and cut. The world

Celebrities like Elizabeth Taylor find owning great gems is glamorous, satisfying, attention-getting, and profitable. The gem-loving actress (left) wears her Cartier necklace and the 33-carat Krupp diamond ring. Best known of her gems is the pear-shaped **Taylor-Burton Diamond** *(page 44).*

The Central Selling Organization (CSO) in London sorts (right), grades, and sells about 70 percent of the world's gem diamonds to international cutting centers. Gemologists color-grade faceted diamonds from "D" (colorless) to "Z" (distinctly yellow), but the CSO has fewer color grades (above) for rough diamonds.

slowly settled on what was once called the *American ideal cut*, now standardized as the *round brilliant* (see page 33). Round brilliants have 58 facets, exactly angled to capture and return the maximum amount of light from the gem to the viewer, producing dazzling effects.

N o other gem material is managed or marketed as diamonds are. Since De Beers gained control of the majority of mine supplies in the 1920s and 1930s and has continued to manage the sale of approximately 70 percent of the world's diamond rough, diamonds have stood apart from the generally chaotic colored gemstone trade as the sole example of tight control and efficient global planning. De Beers usually has had the money and power to make decisions alone—and to make them stick. Its success has been based for decades on convincing producing countries, individual mine operations, rough buyers, cutters, and the rest of the trade and buying public that its control is actually good for the diamond business.

To be sure, the control is not perfect. Once in the 1970s Israeli dealers tried to gain influence over pricing and access to rough diamonds, with a resultant shortage and a huge leap in diamond prices. Declaring such unwarranted price increases bad for the market, De Beers introduced surcharges, forcing the Israelis back in line. In 1992 the civil war in Angola led

Every five weeks the CSO invites its approved list of about 160 buyers (sightholders) to see what diamonds have been selected for them to purchase. Almost all the world's diamonds enter the market through these "sights." For normal goods (under 10.8 carats) there is no haggling. The box is offered "as is," with price and contents not subject to negotiation. Larger diamonds, called "specials," such as the ones on the table (right), are negotiable. Generally De Beers sends tiny diamonds to India, medium sizes to Israel, and larger stones to Antwerp and the U.S. By setting sight prices, the CSO effectively sets the wholesale prices for diamonds. By deciding what goes into each sightholder's box, the CSO determines which part of the diamond business each country receives.

to unprecedented diamond smuggling, which dumped far too many diamonds outside the system. De Beers quietly went into the market, buying enough to stabilize the situation. With the breakup of the Soviet Union, De Beers has had its hands full dealing with Russia, which sells diamonds outside its agreements and refuses to sign long-term contracts.

Before De Beers, diamond prices fluctuated with recessions, supplies, and fads, much as some other gemstones do today. What the syndicate promised was an orderly control of diamond supplies through regular sales at non-negotiated prices. If the trade always knew there would be diamonds available at predictably increasing prices, it could make reasonable business projections. De Beers's control brought market stability.

Buyers share in the win-win plan. Once they think they can flaunt their assets with reasonable bottom-line assurance, they will buy more diamonds. Even through wars and recessions, wholesale diamond prices have outpaced inflation. Except for the rare uncontrolled dip that is usually quickly corrected, diamond buyers have watched the value of their purchases improve. With De Beers's single channel marketing, fine diamonds make shimmering purchases you can wear and enjoy.

De Beers accomplishes this marketing magic by first assuring that most of the world's diamonds move through its system. From its own mines

India facets most diamonds that finish smaller than a quarter carat. Just a few years ago most of that work was done by children using foot-powered laps. Increasingly, a trained work force using electric cutting machines finishes the small goods (above, in Surat). Israel controls costs and quality by utilizing faceting robots (left). A single worker oversees four stations, each of which cuts four diamonds simultaneously. Such Tel Aviv factories facet most marketed diamonds between a quarter and one carat. Larger diamonds, or "specials," such as the 342-carat beauty at Harry Winston, Inc. (lower left) are usually cut in the U.S. Once sawed, the huge rough produced two pear-shaped diamonds. Even minute inclusions, such as the reflected spots below, affect a diamond's clarity grade.

in South Africa to country and individual mine agreements with Russia, Botswana, Namibia, and much of the rest of Africa, the company convinces most mine owners and governments that they are better served selling through the syndicate than on their own. That it markets about 70 percent of the world's rough diamonds (in value) is testimony to De Beers's success. As longtime chairman of De Beers and its parent, Anglo-American Corporation, Harry Oppenheimer told me, "If this is a monopoly, it benefits all concerned: producer, dealer, cutter, jeweler, and consumer."

Once diamonds are unearthed, they are washed, weighed, and sorted for size, color, shape, and quality. Along the way to being set, each stone may be sorted dozens of times. A mine must sort to know what it has before it negotiates a price with De Beers. De Beers grades and sorts before it buys. Parcels of rough diamonds from all over the world are sent by air to London, where De Beers's Central Selling Organization (CSO) handles all sales and transactions with the diamond trade. The CSO determines what world diamond prices will be at the wholesale level and which countries will receive which goods to cut.

About 160 privileged "sightholders," an exclusive group of insiders, receive invitations every five weeks to buy directly from the CSO. Before attending each "sight," they send in a diamond wish list, knowing full well it will not all be granted. In the meantime the CSO gathers and endlessly sorts the rough diamonds into as many as 5,000 categories. Then it assembles small boxes for each sightholder with a computerized list detailing every diamond enclosed. The boxes reflect an ongoing mix of what the sightholder has requested, what the syndicate has in stock, and how De Beers wants to structure the world's diamond trade. This give-and-take protocol is the mechanism by which almost all diamonds enter the market.

Boxes come on a take-it-or-leave-it basis. Except for "specials," rough more than 10.8 carats, there is no negotiation on box content or price.

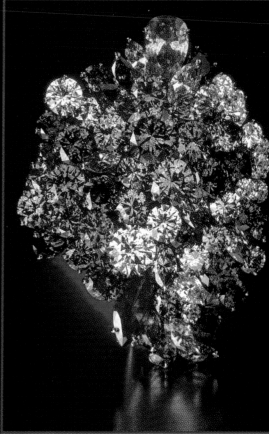

Many diamonds that are colored and colorless under room light (right) fluoresce under ultraviolet light (above), a beautiful as well as useful identification phenomenon. Under a microscope an unfaceted diamond (below) reveals the triangular details of its crystalline growth.

Diamond pin by Chip Clark, Smithsonian Institution (2)

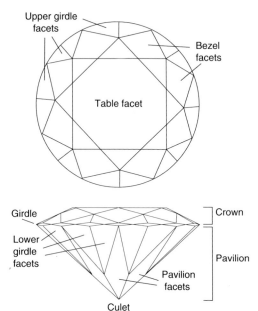

Upper girdle facets
Bezel facets
Table facet
Girdle
Crown
Lower girdle facets
Pavilion
Pavilion facets
Culet

Diamond grading is rigidly structured. Most dealers want round brilliants, with 58 facets, standardized crown and pavilion angles, and ideal table proportions. When the Gemological Institute of America's color and clarity grading systems were introduced in the 1930s, they became practically the world standard. The highest colorless grade is "D," and each new letter to "Z" indicates more yellow. A color grade near "D" means greater rarity and a higher price. Eleven GIA clarity grades (judged at 10X magnification) cover all diamonds from "Flawless" to three "Imperfect" grades with visible inclusions.

GIA Color Grading Scale

D E F	G H I J	K L M	N O P Q R	S T U V W X Y Z	
Colorless	Near colorless	Faint yellow	Very light yellow	Light yellow	Fancy yellow

GIA Clarity Grading Scale

F	IF	VVS$_1$ VVS$_2$	VS$_1$ VS$_2$	SI$_1$ SI$_2$	I$_1$ I$_2$ I$_3$
Flawless	Internally flawless	Very, very slight inclusions	Very slight inclusions	Slight inclusions	Imperfect

If a sightholder refuses his prepared box, he might be invited back only once or twice. If he accepts, he has to pay in full within 7 to 10 days and arrange for shipping. The average purchase by each sightholder at each of the 10 annual sights is about $2.9 million, totaling near $4.64 billion a year.

Who gets which rough diamonds actually determines who will be in the diamond business. That aspect of CSO control, often overlooked by all but diamond insiders, is how De Beers has worked with various counties to build an industry. Before World War II the diamond trade was largely a Jewish business centered almost exclusively in Europe and the U.S. Cutters and dealers on the Continent either fled or were killed, permanently disabling diamond centers like Amsterdam.

After the war De Beers restructured the diamond world. Generally they gave New York dealers the largest rough and best colors because the U.S. had the cutting skills as well as the market. De Beers made a gigantic gift to the new country, Israel, reserving for it much of the rough between a quarter and one carat, thereby instantly establishing an Israeli diamond industry. India typically got the rough under a quarter carat, "melee,"

Diamond clubs, or **bourses,** *around the world provide safe areas, private rooms for important deals, and anonymity for buying and selling gems. With billions of dollars in annual sales, the Antwerp bourse is busiest (left), whereas Tel Aviv's (right) is liveliest.*

used for small accent stones. Antwerp received unusually-configured rough because its skilled cutters were best at transforming the material into "fancy" shapes, such as marquise and hearts. That distribution held until recently when Thailand, Hong Kong, China, and Japan got into the market as cutters and consumers. When U.S. and European recessions slowed sales, De Beers began targeting the emerging Asian nations as future markets, advertising with U.S.-style campaigns, and diverting more rough to Asian sightholders. With Asian economies now in a slump, De Beers will adjust once more.

Diamonds are forever" now romances young lovers in Shanghai and Tokyo, just as it has American couples since the 1940s. Spending more than $100 million a year on U.S. advertising alone, De Beers has raised consumer awareness to the point where more than 70 percent of American brides receive diamonds. Before the De Beers advertising campaign, Japan had no diamond-buying history. In just over two decades De Beers has stimulated sales to where the same percentage of Japanese brides receive diamonds. By the early 1990s, with only half the U.S. population, Japan bought $2.1 billion of diamonds annually, compared to $2.7 billion spent by the United States.

Southeast Asia was responsible for most 1980s' diamond market growth. As Thailand and Hong Kong became more important jewelry centers, they increasingly wanted to supply their factories with diamonds cut locally for less. The shift to Asia worried cutters and dealers in traditional centers like Tel Aviv, Bombay, and Antwerp, who saw their own markets threatened by lower labor costs. Then, in 1997 several Asian economies staggered, slowing gem and jewelry factory output and sales. A significant Asian exception has been India. Because of expanded partnerships and contracts with Australia's Argyle mine, Indian diamond cutters and jewelry manufacturers are enjoying unprecedented growth.

One thing is certain. Diamond prosperity depends on skilled labor in various countries, as well as prosperous economies that produce large numbers of consumers with disposable incomes. After nearly 3000 years, the diamond, this grand old jewel, remains at the center of today's swirling gem and jewelry activity.

JEWELS AND ARTIFACTS

G reat gemstones are like fine wine, revered philosophers, good friends, and old stories. They get better with age. But unlike their venerated associates with finite lives, diamonds may very well last forever. The crystals themselves cannot be dated. Only encapsulated datable materials trapped inside during its creation disclose a diamond's birth date. The ones thus far dated indicate ages between 600 million and 3.5 billion years. There is no doubt that some diamonds younger and some older are awaiting discovery, because the conditions that formed diamonds existed when the earth's crust cooled and still exist today.

The reason gems become artifacts has a great deal to do with their structure and characteristics: beauty, durability, and rarity—and therefore, value. Only the most stressful circumstance, such as war or a natural disaster, would cause an owner to leave or relinquish such treasures. Far more typical is for one generation to safeguard and pass down gems, using them as a link between generations or dynasties. And as gemstones typically retain their polish, color, and value, they deserve our trust. Fine diamonds make quintessential heirlooms.

Since we generally think of diamonds as colorless, it is surprising how many of the great diamond artifacts are yellow, pink, blue, orange, brown, green, or red. Diamonds are also the most likely of all gems to have distinctive or descriptive names. By personalizing diamonds, people reveal their special reverence for these incredible crystals. In 1959 Harry Winston bought a 30.82-carat diamond then known as the *Eugénie Blue*, which cereal heiress Marjorie Merriweather Post purchased in a ring. After she donated her treasure to the Smithsonian Institution in 1964, curators discovered the jewel was named in error. It never belonged to the French empress. Now renamed the *Blue Heart* (see page 4), it and the *Hope*, two of the greatest blue diamonds in history, were owned and publicly worn by a pair of Washington *grande dames*, and both gems are now on view in adjoining museum rooms.

The opulent gem-encrusted Nadir Throne is but one of three thrones in Tehran. Eighty-eight inches high (2.25 meters), its wooden structure is overlaid with enameled gold and studded with hundreds of gems. Diamonds 10 to 25 carats decorate the throne's front and backrest.

Bank Markazi Jomhouri Islami Iran

Diamond arrays by Chip Clark, Smithsonian Institution (2)

Large, important gems leave a trail of intrigue, lore, and mystery through history. The spectacular pink rectangular table-shaped *Dari-i-Nur* (Sea of Light), estimated at 185 carats, today is part of the Crown Jewels of Iran (see page 5). But no less a source than 17th century traveler, writer, gem fancier, and dealer Jean Baptiste Tavernier described a fabulous jewel in India that he called the *Great Table*. Most observers believe the two are the same and that the treasure was part of the loot carried away by Nadir Shah after the sack of Delhi in 1739. Various Persian rulers wore it in public in the 1800s as did the last Shah of Iran, who donned the *Dari-i-Nur* as a cap decoration during his 1967 coronation.

While in Delhi, Nadir Shah finessed another of history's great prizes. A 186-carat diamond was first reported in 1304, owned by India's Rajah of Malwa. Next it was seen in the possession of Mogul Emperor Baber

Colored diamonds fascinate visitors in Smithsonian's newly renovated gem hall (above). Included are the **Blue Heart,** *the intense yellow* **Shephard** *and colorless* **Pearson** *as well as unnamed pink, cognac, yellow, and green dazzlers. Janet Annenberg Hooker donated 50 matched starburst-cut fancy-yellow diamonds set by Cartier into a necklace, with 25.3 carat ear clips, and a 61.12-carat ring (opposite). Holland's Max Drukker plucked this black beauty from a De Beers parcel of industrial diamonds and faceted it into the 33.74-carat* **Star of Amsterdam** *(right).*

and passed to subsequent emperors for two centuries. When Nadir Shah stormed in from Persia, the last Mogul emperor to possess the diamond successfully hid it from the conqueror for days, until a concubine revealed that the ruler wore it in his turban. Nadir Shah devised a plan to get the gem without having to kill the emperor. Relying on an Oriental custom, Nadir planned a feast for the emperor. During dinner he suggested they exchange turbans, a courtesy not to be refused. Leaving the banquet, Nadir unrolled the turban, spilling out the huge gem. "Koh-i-noor," he is said to have gasped. "Mountain of Light!" And the storied jewel had a name.

Unfortunately for the Persians, Nadir's heirs squabbled over the diamond until it landed in the jewel chamber in Lahore, capital of Punjab, just before the British annexed the state. The East India Company seized the gem to present to Queen Victoria in 1850. Disappointed by its lack of fire,

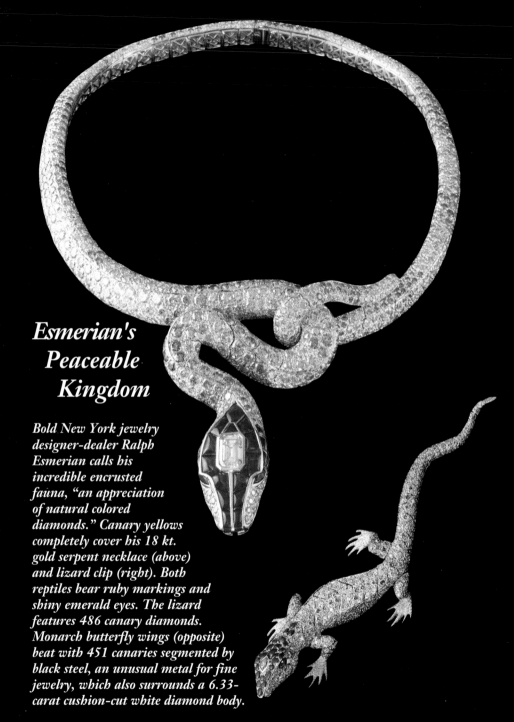

Esmerian's Peaceable Kingdom

Bold New York jewelry designer-dealer Ralph Esmerian calls his incredible encrusted fauna, "an appreciation of natural colored diamonds." Canary yellows completely cover his 18 kt. gold serpent necklace (above) and lizard clip (right). Both reptiles bear ruby markings and shiny emerald eyes. The lizard features 486 canary diamonds. Monarch butterfly wings (opposite) beat with 451 canaries segmented by black steel, an unusual metal for fine jewelry, which also surrounds a 6.33-carat cushion-cut white diamond body.

A pink diamond menagerie would have been a "totally impossible" fantasy before Australia's Argyle Mine, which produces most of the world's pinks. The flamingo pin contains 900 round and 188 marquise and pear-shape diamonds. Dreamy pink elephants become a reality with Esmerian's unique mother and baby pin (top right), decorated with more than 630 pinks (20.65 carats), 10 rubies, and black steel tusks.

Royalty and gems have been on intimate terms since the first king thought he would look better wearing rare and wonderful jewels. Eastern potentates favored a unique adornment, a jiqa, or aigrette (left), which was used as the center of interest on turbans or other headdresses. The various Persian shahs showed particular fondness for such decorations.

After Harry Winston bought Frederick the Great's jeweled agate box, he discovered the various "pink" diamonds on the 1740 treasure (right) were enhanced by the addition of rose-colored foil tucked beneath the larger stones.

Bank Markazi Jomhouri Islami Iran

Harry Winston collection

she ordered it recut to a brighter but smaller 108.93-carat centerpiece, which adorned the crowns of subsequent British queens. The Queen Mother still enjoys it on state occasions as the premier jewel in her 1937 coronation crown.

Although the *Koh-i-noor* is justifiably famous—even infamous, Americans generally consider the *Hope* the best known and most recognizable diamond in the world (see cover). The *Hope's* long dramatic history is preceded by great gaps and mystery. Found and originally cut in India, the stunning 112-carat blue gem enjoyed a spectacular regal entrance into Europe. Jean Baptiste Tavernier returned from the subcontinent in 1668 with it as the focal point of his Indian diamond collection. After hearing Tavernier's stories, Louis XIV bought 45 large and 1,122 small diamonds for more than $300,000. He designated the main jewel *The Blue Diamond of the Crown*, a name which rapidly evolved into the *French Blue*. From there the great blue's history took bizarre turns.

To the delight of Marie Antoinette and other ladies of the court, the king's goldsmith in 1673 recut the *French Blue* into a brilliant 67-carat heart. Then, along with a number of other treasures, the premier gem of the French

42

Crown Jewels was stolen in 1792, and never recovered!

Almost four decades later, in London, a strange thing happened. An unusual irregularly cut 45.52-carat diamond appeared and somehow looked familiar. People who remembered the *French Blue* thought it too much of a coincidence that two large blue diamonds were so similar. Although no direct connection was ever made nor a thief apprehended, it is still assumed that the 67-carat *French Blue* was recut to the 45.52-carat gem offered for sale.

The great blue assumed yet another new owner and a new name. British banker Henry Thomas Hope bought the gem for $90,000 and, even though it changed hands often, the *Hope* retained his name. The diamond stayed in Hope's family until 1906 when Lord Francis Hope encountered financial difficulties. Over the next five years the *Hope* was bought and sold several more times, including once to the Sultan of Turkey. Then Pierre Cartier bought the *Hope* in Paris and sold it in 1911 to Washington socialite Evalyn Walsh McLean for $154,000.

For the next thirty-six years Mrs. McLean cherished wearing the *Hope* at parties and benefits around Washington. With what passed for safety, she occasionally hid the gem in armchair upholstery. After her death, Harry Winston bought her estate gems in 1949, paying $179,920 for the *Hope*. Later, in 1958, Winston donated the deep blue diamond to the American people and placed it on permanent display at the Smithsonian Institution.

The disposition of the *French Blue* and the apparent missing pieces have captured the attention of gemological sleuths for two centuries. A Goya portrait painted in 1799 shows Spain's Queen Maria Luisa wearing a gem that looks remarkably like the *Hope*. If so, that suggests that the *French Blue*, stolen in 1792, was recut soon afterward and at least three new blue gems from it were sold in Spain. Karl II, Duke of Brunswick, later bought a 6-carat blue; and Edwin Streeter, a British gem expert, purchased a one-carat blue in 1877, which he called the *Pirie*. Of all the blue diamonds examined while looking for *French Blue* remnants, these two are the most likely to be authentic. It is unknown where either of these gems is today.

One realization should now be clear. From the beginning of human history, owning great gems has been the prerogative of rulers. Kings and queens usually had the wealth and power to buy or seize jewels. Many realms even restricted ownership of gems to royals and their courts. Then the Industrial Revolution and subsequent rise of democracies led to a decline of monarchies. Over the last century, great capitalistic barons and other wealthy commoners gradually replaced many of the world's royals as buyers of expensive gems and jewelry. "Financial or business royalty" is what New York gem dealer Ralph Esmerian calls the new clients. "Wealthy Mideast and Asian customers buy because a love of color and great gems is part of their lifestyle. Then there is the snobbery of showing you can afford the best. Americans just don't seem to need that splendor. It's not in our blood."

Even the Queen of England would likely find little public support today for gathering more jewels. Today's subjects expect rulers to be socially conscious and frugal. The oil rich Middle Eastern rulers who lavished money on gems, cars, and palaces two or three decades ago maintain much lower

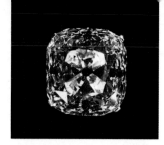

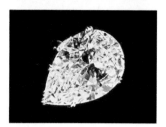

Great diamonds have names to honor a person, place, or thought. Because they sparkle, diamonds often are called "stars." New York's Baumgold Brothers faceted the 111-carat **Earth Star** *(above). The 128-carat* **Tiffany Diamond** *(top left) remains on display in the New York store. Although the 62.42-carat* **Taylor-Burton** *(center left) had at least 4 previous owners, it is now linked to the acting pair. The 205-carat* **Red Cross Diamond's** *name serves double duty, to describe its cut and to honor the charity (bottom left).*

profiles today. I do not mean that royals are not buying jewelry. Of course they are. But when fabulous stones enter the market, the more likely buyer is a newly rich industrialist or a museum. The best known gem buying ruler at the moment is the Sultan of Brunei, who apparently is accumulating the largest private jewel collection in the world.

Another trend seems to be growing. More and more great gems are going into public collections. Recently, knowing I was to be in Europe to research gems and make new photographs of private collections, a group contacted me to look for a fine, preferably unnamed diamond to be the main piece in a new museum collection. The museum was willing to spend up to $10 million for the gem. It had already searched for months without success. In Switzerland I saw what I considered the ideal diamond: 65 carats, D-flawless, unnamed—perfect in every way—except over their budget at $14 million. The owners of the fantastic gem had already had it on the market for months but had not sold it to any of the obvious buyers. A few years earlier Harry Winston or one of the Mideast oil family members would have

44

At 968.80 carats, the Star of Sierra Leone (top) was the third largest diamond ever found. It yielded 17 gems, the largest being a 53.96-carat pear-shape. Believed to have been part of the Czarist Crown Jewels, the 102-carat Ashberg Diamond (above left) sold to a private collector in Europe after World War II. On display in the Smithsonian Institution's remarkable world-class gem collection, is the highly fluorescent 127.01-carat Portuguese Diamond (above, right).

immediately captured such a prize. Now the price seemed strangely out of phase. A new museum was the only current bidder, and even it could not raise the asking price. So the diamond remained unsold.

Which jewels become collectibles? Few diamonds smaller than 20 carats are significant enough to merit a special designation, unless they have a distinctive color. Even with the Argyle mine, most experts feel there are no more than 20 or so authenticated natural red diamonds. A few years ago an imperfect, irregularly cut small red diamond came into the market—only .93 carats. Still, at auction it fetched $1 million plus commission, more than a million dollars a carat. Rarity is the stuff of collectibility.

O ne in a million" is what the diamond trade calls a collection-quality gem. In reality, such diamonds are far rarer than that. For decades the Gemological Institute of America (GIA) has kept records on both diamond production and on the stones it receives for grading. The current annual world diamond production is estimated at 110 to 120 million carats. But of those, only two to two and a half million carats produce faceted diamonds larger than one carat in the desired D to H colors, flawless to SI_2 clarity grades. In other words, of all the diamonds mined, only a fiftieth have the size, color, and clarity that buyers want. Despite the huge productions of Australia and Zaire, about 90 percent of those desirable two million carats (which, once faceted, will amount to considerably less than one million carats) come from just 5 countries (in production order); Botswana, Russia, South Africa, Namibia, and Angola.

Large D-flawless diamonds (those with the best color and clarity grades) are among the rarest materials on earth. According to GIA's astounding estimate, no more than 600 such crystals a year finish between one to two carats. In fact all D-color diamonds are rare, even when they have microscopic inclusions. Fewer than 5,000 D-color diamonds larger than half a carat are found a year. Only large high-quality colored diamonds are scarcer. If every finished carat requires moving 250 tons of earth, to retrieve a two-carat D-flawless diamond necessitates moving a mountain.

Cloaked in mystery, the great pink, yellow, and blue diamonds were believed to contain mystical powers. Rulers with all the wealth imaginable did not actually need another treasure. But they did need to believe in their own divinity and to display visible proof of their great personal dominance. It was easy for them to assume the implied strength inherent in the great colored stones to feel personally protected from harm. So strong was royal faith in the power of gems that kings risked their lives, their fortunes, and even their kingdoms by going to war for more.

There is another aspect of gems that Americans seldom consider that was extremely important to ancient rulers. It is a consideration kept current in more troubled areas of the world. Gemstones are the most compact, portable, universal, negotiable of all valuables. For a ruler, three of the four traditional forms of wealth (land, people, gems, and precious metals) were remarkably unwieldy and unlikely to be transported far or fast. But gems small enough to hide in a pocket or purse could support a fleeing monarch for decades. Today's refugees continue the practice whenever possible.

As part of its 100-year celebration, De Beers cut the 273-carat **Centenary Diamond** *from a 599-carat rough recovered from South Africa's Premier Mine. The company describes the unusually shaped gem as "the largest modern-cut top-color flawless diamond in the world."*

Paper money, stocks, homes, and property can all be worthless during crises. No one knows how many Russian immigrants continue to arrive in Israel with diamonds sewn into the hems of their coats.

I once did the calculations to visualize portability. Assuming the need to move a million dollars across borders, if you had a million one-dollar bills, the stacks would fill about 42 cubic feet and weigh nearly a ton. A million dollar gold brick (with gold at $400 an ounce) might be difficult to carry or hide at 135 pounds. But with 142 carats to an ounce, the 65-carat D-flawless diamond I described on page 44 weighs less than half an ounce, yet was valued at $14 million!

Gems offer several benefits not found in other, more typical investments. There is the personal satisfaction of buying to enjoy what you own and giving to ones you love. Automobiles, fur coats, boats, and clothing are all relatively short-term satisfactions; they will deteriorate over time. In contrast, diamonds are already hundreds of millions to billions of years old—traditional symbols of wealth and beauty, timeless symbols of love and eternity. The precious crystals are not even an earthly exclusive. Tiny diamonds occasionally arrive in meteors, and diamonds have been detected as dust between galaxies. Think of diamonds as our link to the universe. Born within the earth beginning when our planet was young, they are tangible evidence of nature's perfection. Diamonds are stars we can hold in our hands.

SYNTHETIC AND INDUSTRIAL DIAMONDS

Just before the turn of the century, one of the most enduring of all dreams came true for a lone scientist working in his Paris laboratory. Auguste Verneuil achieved what most thought impossible: he took bags of the common chemicals aluminum oxide and chromium, and with a remarkably simple flame-fusion process, transformed them into rubies. The achievement only heightened interest in climbing the Mt. Everest of gem synthesis, making diamonds. Half a century, millions of dollars, and a great many scientists later, General Electric announced it had combined high temperature and high pressure to replicate the conditions 100 miles underground: G.E. began transforming carbon into industrial diamonds in the 1950s.

Diamond dealers fretted that growing diamonds would collapse the natural gem trade. General Electric did make some gem and near-gem diamonds (see page 51), but they cost more to produce than naturals sold for at the time. The market for synthetics turned out to be industrial diamonds. A world only recently released from the miseries of World War II had expanding economies not only in North America but also in Europe and Asia. Rebuilding factories and industries meant vastly increased needs for grinding tools, and nothing else was as good as diamonds for abrasives.

The earliest Indian cutters more than two thousand years ago determined that only other diamonds could saw or shape their diamond gems. For many other tasks, ruby or sapphire grit, called *emery*, served well. The manufacturing demands of World War II swelled the number of factories throughout the industrialized world, creating explosive demands for diamonds for cutting, sawing, grinding, and polishing hard materials.

All diamond mines except those in Namibia produce more industrial-grade diamonds than gems. In areas like Australia and Zaire the percentage of industrial diamonds soars. What the development of synthetic diamonds by G.E., De Beers, and others in several countries achieved was to provide a reliable and inexpensive source at the exact time when industrial

Almost all modern industrial processes require diamonds for cutting and polishing. Even high-end art glass maker Steuben relies on diamond-tipped pens for engraving its one-of-a-kind designs in lead crystal.

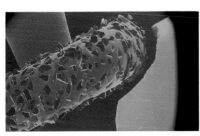

diamond use soared. By 1980 more than half the diamonds consumed each year came from a factory and not from the ground. De Beers became G.E.'s biggest competitor in synthetics. Soon the Soviet Union, Japan, and Korea entered the field, gaining valuable experience that served them well as technology changed in the 1990s.

Synthetic diamonds provided several benefits. They were relatively fast and inexpensive to produce. More importantly, they eliminated the fear that had plagued the Allies throughout World War II, a loss of diamond supplies during periods of great manufacturing needs. Synthetics also were available in more consistent sizes and shapes than naturals, making them easier to incorporate into tools. Since industrial diamonds are almost never seen by the public, the fact they are usually yellow and included is inconsequential. Except when industries needed larger diamonds for special dies, cutting tools, and oil rig drill bits (above), they switched from naturals to synthetics for the majority of their grinding tasks.

Diamonds for pennies was the result. As synthetic production increased, people found new uses for industrials. Dentists moved from all steel to disposable diamond-tipped drills (top left), which proved to be cooler, faster, safer, and more comfortable for patients. Almost everything that needs polishing perfectly (piston rings, optics, contact lenses, glasses, precision

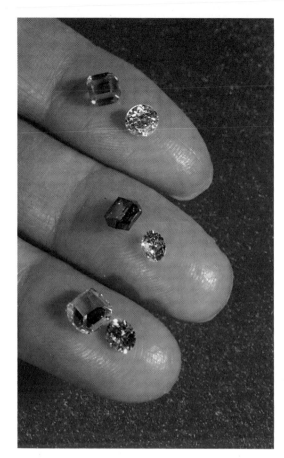

Natural diamonds usually perform large grinding tasks, such as oil drilling (opposite). Synthetic diamonds can just as easily cut teeth as groove highways (opposite). Although it was the first to make gem quality diamonds (left), G.E. never sold them. Chatham Created Gems has contracted with Russia to market its single crystal synthetics as gems. The Russian crystals emerge from furnaces as almost perfectly shaped pre-forms ready for cutting (above).

tools) can be done with synthetics. Simple tasks like grooving highways (page 50), cutting construction and decorative stones (page 53), and faceting other gemstones could then be done faster and less expensively with synthetic diamonds. Most of those early tasks utilized only diamond's hardness.

Other superlative diamond qualities are perfect for high-tech heat management and optical applications. Nothing else transmits heat as fast or as well. And diamond is also stable to temperatures near 1000°C. Engineers have produced diamond thermometers to work reliably near absolute zero and to operate in satellite telescopes measuring the almost undetectable amount of heat generated by individual stars (see page 53).

As electronic components decreased in size and increased in power, moving heat from sensitive parts became a top priority. Early communications satellites incorporated microscopic diamond cubes to keep tiny transistors cool (see page 52). This ability to move heat efficiently is a core factor in yet another new diamonds business.

A different, extremely valuable characteristic makes diamonds one of the most exciting of all research materials. Diamond passes virtually the entire electromagnetic spectrum without interference. Many substances are transparent to visible light; glass, quartz, colorless sapphire, etc. But visible light is just a thin band in the spectrum. This means when windows covering

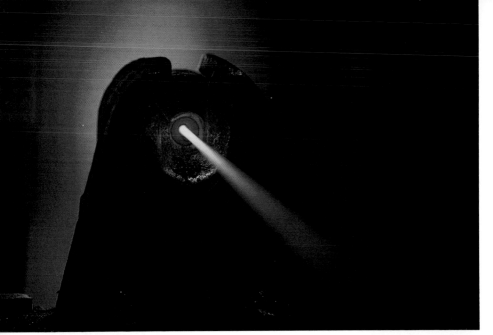

Perfect filament diameters result when hot oversized wire is pulled through a diamond die (above). A precisely shaped crystal forms the world's sharpest eye scalpel (left), which retains its diamond-hard edge after repeated use. Minute internal diamond cubes (right) transfer heat away from sensitive electronic satellite components.

sensitive instruments must let in various critical wavelengths and remain clean and unabraded in hostile environments, diamonds are the logical choice. Who needs such windows? Mainly industry, the military, and space agencies. When an aircraft or tank, for example, has to determine if a visitor is friend or foe, it relies on sensors. A missile racing through low altitude desert conditions may require heat or radar wavelengths to find its mark. In all cases, tiny amounts of information must pass unimpeded through a window and into a sensor. The window of choice is diamond.

Until recently, diamonds large enough to be useful as windows, thermometers, and heat sinks were naturals, and relatively expensive. Breakthrough technology that began in the U.S. in the 1960s and came alive in the 1980s promises to be the revolutionary basis for window, tool, and heat management industries in the 1990s. Early diamond synthesis from G.E., Japan's Sumitomo, De Beers, and the Russians used high temperature and pressure to grow single crystal diamonds. Now all eyes and a lot of research money are on a new low pressure technique, chemical vapor deposition (CVD), that promises to coat almost anything with diamonds. Methane or

Stone sawing consumes huge volumes of industrial diamonds. Using circular, reciprocating, and wire saws, workers extract manageable slabs or blocks that are used for decoration and construction. On Canada's Ogden Mountain, Kirk Makepeace slices boulders at the world's largest jade mine (above). Utilizing diamond's unsurpassed heat conductivity, a diamond slice (right), destined for the eyepiece of a space telescope, measures the temperatures of single stars.

acetylene gas usually provides the carbon source. When the gas mixture is right, and the temperatures of the flame (or other heat source) and the recipient are balanced, microscopic crystals scatter over the object, coating it with a thin diamond film.

Two of the earliest commercial items attempted were razor blades for a lifetime edge and faceted cubic zirconia (the imitation diamond) to see if buyers could be fooled. This almost unknown CVD industry quickly flourished to where it already accounts for the majority of Sumitomo's $400 million annual synthetic diamond sales.

CVD diamonds are made by De Beers, G.E., Norton, Raytheon, Crystallume, Diamonex, Sumitomo, and about 200 companies and educational researchers, including CVD pioneer John Angus at Case Western Reserve University, who sees his 1960s dream coming true. The business seems to be dividing into three areas: coating cutting tools to make them harder, creating large transparent windows, and managing heat. Still in the "products looking for a market" stage, CVD is as wide open as its creators' imaginations.

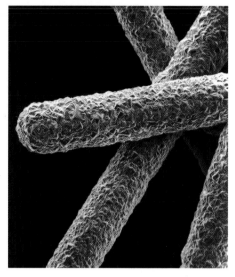

Chemical vapor deposition (CVD), the newest synthesis technology, exploits several of diamond's most useful characteristics; hardness, wavelength transparency, thermal conductivity, and resistance to mechanical wear and chemical corrosion. Created in low-pressure plasma reactors, thin layers of diamond crystals coat everyday items to make them diamond-hard (opposite, far right). Large, transparent windows (opposite, top) have vital defense, space, and industrial sensor applications. New diamond CVD substrates even cool computer chips (opposite, bottom). Strong and stiff, diamond tubes (below), made by depositing tiny diamond crystals on tungsten coils of any shape, safely carry high-temperature or dangerous gases or liquids.

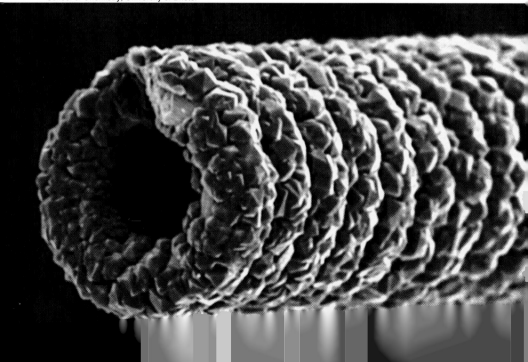

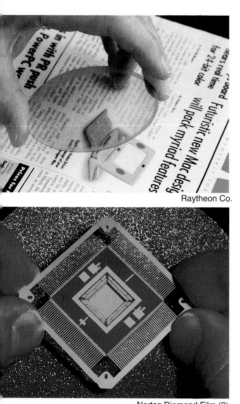

Raytheon Co.

Norton Diamond Film (2)

Coating for hardness was an obvious first step. Drill bits and all other items that might once have used industrial diamonds are being tested. A sunglass line promotes scratchproof lenses, but the coating is really diamondlike and not diamond. Wire dies and cutting tools are already in use. High- and low-tech tools are all potential products. While dreaming of other uses, imagine a scratchproof, rustproof diamond-coated automobile.

Companies already make diamond windows in unprecedented sizes, 5 inches or more across (above). This is polycrystalline material as yet unsuitable for gems. The first Venus space probe window was a large, expensive natural single-crystal diamond slice. Future windows will surely be from diamond CVD.

Heat is the enemy of electronic components. Computer chips can be almost microscopic yet operate at supercomputer speeds if the heat they generate is removed. CVD diamond coatings can transfer heat harmlessly. One researcher predicts a 4-inch all-diamond-coated computer will run faster than a Cray, without the need for the supercomputer's refrigeration unit. For now, single computer chips rest on thin CVD diamond squares (above).

There are legitimate gem trade concerns about future developments in high-temperature high-pressure single-crystal growth. Russia has become a major producer of synthetic gem diamonds. Though most crystals are still yellow, Russia is growing enough near-colorless diamonds to worry dealers. When small faceted goods are mixed into parcels of natural diamonds, Russian synthetics are difficult for buyers to detect.

BUYING AND CARING

O f all the major gemstones, diamonds are at once the most available and the most difficult to learn how to buy. When you find an attractive colored stone, you can usually decide on the basis of beauty alone. However, diamonds are graded and priced on totally different standards that may seem confusing. With a few diamond basics, you can shop with competence and safety.

Study the two grading charts on page 33, which represent half the famous "4 Cs" used to value diamonds; color, clarity, carat weight, and cut. Note there are 23 finely drawn, almost imperceptible letter-grade distinctions between colorless and yellow. Even though you may not be able to see the minute differences between one or two letter grades for color, someone could and did before your diamond was priced. It is not necessary to be able to grade diamonds or even recognize each color. But knowing the grading concept and what the letters stand for will probably save you money. Also look at the 11 clarity grades. The range covers diamonds from flawless—those with absolutely nothing visible in or on them at 10X magnification—to imperfect stones with easy-to-see inclusions. Every up or down move in color or clarity results in price jumps of hundreds to thousands of dollars.

Now you know the framework jewelers use to buy diamonds. Next, deal with retailers by using common sense and asking a few good questions. Diamonds have an almost universal global wholesale price. De Beers in effect standardizes this by selling 70 percent of all rough diamonds to cutters and dealers at the same carat cost. Brisk competition means that faceted diamonds arrive to jewelers at very similar prices and have a lower retail markup than almost any other gemstone. Since costs are much the same among jewelers, real bargain prices are unlikely. *Most price differences are the result of misgrading color and clarity.* Be sensible and cautious. Comparison shopping broadens your choices and familiarizes you with the market.

Price reflects rarity. Very few diamonds have both the perfect colorless color, "D," and perfect clarity, "Flawless." A large 12.95-carat D-flawless diamond, like the one in this Tiffany ring, is among the rarest of all gems. Only fancy-colored diamonds are more expensive.

Buying gems and jewelry is highly personal. Taste, style, and money are all factors. Diamonds do not age, but cut and settings can. New York's 47th Street (above) claims wholesale prices to the public, which is impossible. Learn diamond fundamentals to be an informed shopper. And consider custom jewelry like the pieces opposite to assure owning and enjoying treasures suited to your needs.

Widely advertised diamond prices are often confusing. When the price for a one-carat H-SI$_1$ gem varies by a thousand dollars, obviously something is wrong. Either buy from someone you trust and can come back to or become an educated customer, or both. Most problems arise from retailers overstating a diamond's true color and clarity. This is actually easy to check. For larger diamonds, get a lab report. In the trade the GIA still sets the standard for grading. Your jeweler can send your stone to GIA or one of several other gem labs, such as European Gemological Laboratories in the USA, or to a respected lab in Europe or Thailand. Any important diamond you are interested in may already have been graded. If your jeweler does not have a lab report for the diamond you like, that does not mean it is not a good gem; it merely means that whoever owns the gem has not paid to have it graded. You can insist on a lab report as part of your sale, or you can have the jeweler guarantee the stone's color, clarity, and weight in writing. Later you can have your diamond independently graded and appraised at the same time.

Buying a diamond is unlike any other expensive purchase. The nuances that determine the gem's value are usually known to the seller and almost never fully understood by the buyer. More and more diamonds are clarity enhanced with a glass-like filler to obscure cracks or fissures. Such treatment should be disclosed to the customer. The Federal Trade Commission, in its latest gem guidelines, did no favors for consumers when it declared that laser drilling does not have to be disclosed. I think all such treatments *must* be disclosed. Dark inclusions and other discolored areas in diamonds can

Lelia Hendren collection

be bleached after laser drilling, leaving tiny but visible hollow drill holes from the surface to the spots. These drill holes can also be "glass-filled."

Proportion affects price. "Spread" cuts, making diamonds too wide and too shallow, give the impression of larger gems, but diminish brilliance. Poorly cut diamonds produce "windows," which leak light rather than reflect it to the viewer. Badly cut girdles and facets that do not line up are "cut" considerations that reduce the value of a gem.

Diamond prices are based on all four "Cs." Individual taste will determine whether you consider color, clarity, cut, or size most important. Diamonds over two carats are considerably rarer than smaller ones and may cost four times as much as one carat gems. Assuming comparable quality, the larger the gem, the higher the price per carat.

Are diamonds forever? They can be with care. Compared to buying diamonds, caring for them is easy. One of the enduring misconceptions is that because they are the hardest known substance, they must also be indestructible. Not true. Diamonds can break because they have cleavage planes. Unfortunately, just the right blow at a sensitive point can chip or split a gem. Most owners who have broken stones in rings have hit them just wrong against sinks, counters, cars, or walls. Remove diamond jewelry during hard physical work or play. Be careful with rings since they are most vulnerable. Check mounts regularly to be sure your stones are secure.

The greatest need for regular diamond care is cleaning. See page 62 for cleaning tips. Finally, protect your diamond by having it appraised regularly and fully insured. Your diamond is already millions to billions of years old. With regular care you can proudly pass it to your children and they to theirs. Consider these most desirable of all gems permanent gifts of nature.

Floral Flights
of Fancy

When price is no object, elaborate and personal custom designs make wonderful lifelong treasures. Naturalistic designs are historic favorites with jewelers. Fancy colored diamonds mixed with other colored gems are ideal for depicting flora with charming results. Van Cleef & Arpels specializes in such pieces, from its 1940s four-inch (10.3 cm) high palm tree brooch to a contemporary multicolored bracelet (opposite) as well as daffodil and gardenia pins and earrings.

Advantages of Diamonds

Color—any color is possible, although colorless and near-colorless sell best. Fancy colors are collection favorites.
Rarity—sufficiently rare and controlled to maintain value.
Durability—the hardest known material.
Beauty—highest refractive index, most sparkle of major gems.
History—the grandest of all gems; great stones are named.
Birthstone—April

Caring for Diamonds

Home cleaning—warm water and detergent; vodka with soft brush.
Ultrasonic or Steamer—generally safe. Diamonds attract grease and skin oil. The key to cleaning diamonds is to physically remove such oils.
Setting—as with all fine gemstones, diamonds should be set only by skilled workers. Although unsurpassed in hardness, diamonds do cleave, so they can be broken by sharp blows. Avoid direct contact with jewelers' torches.
Storing—because diamonds will scratch anything including each other, store them in cloth or boxes, separated from other gems and precious metals. With care, diamonds are indeed forever.

Although diamonds are the most standardized and controlled commodity in the gem world, most individuals buy few in a lifetime, usually one at a time. Buying wisely requires that you become an informed consumer. Familiarize yourself with color, clarity, and cut grading since extremely minor variations mean large price differences. Avoid purported bargains and "wholesale" pricing. For years of satisfaction, find a dealer you trust, and plan to pay a fair price.

G emstones are sold by weight, not by size or volume. This significant difference makes them more like gold and silver than other luxury products, such as furs, yachts, automobiles, or watches. Since gems are comprised of different chemical elements, they do not all weigh the same. Therefore, gemologists use weight as one means of identification.

Weight, or density, is expressed as specific gravity (SG). Diamond has an SG of 3.52, which means a diamond weighs 3.52 times as much as the same volume of water. In comparison, emeralds are lighter, with an SG of 2.72. Because each gem has its own specific gravity, gem sizes vary considerably compared with other stones of the same weight. With equal weights, emeralds are larger than diamonds; rubies and sapphires are smaller.

Gems are weighed in carats (not to be confused with "karat," which refers to the purity of gold). A carat, from the ancient Indian use of carob seeds for small consistent weights, equals 1/5 gram, or 1/142 ounce. Sizes are measured in millimeters (see below). A round one carat diamond, a standard weight in the trade, is typically 6.5mm in diameter. A round one carat ruby or sapphire, being denser, measures about 6.1mm across; a round one carat emerald is usually 6.6 to 6.7mm.

Cutting proportions for diamonds are normally much more standardized than for colored gems. When buying diamonds, the main factors that determine price are the four Cs: carat weight, color (or lack of color), clarity, and cut. When in doubt, consult an expert. With diamonds, it pays.

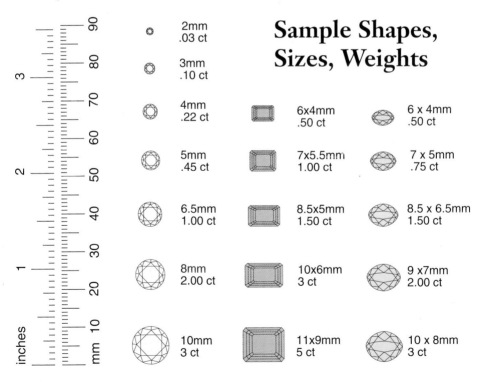

Sample Shapes, Sizes, Weights

2mm .03 ct			
3mm .10 ct			
4mm .22 ct	6x4mm .50 ct	6 x 4mm .50 ct	
5mm .45 ct	7x5.5mm 1.00 ct	7 x 5mm .75 ct	
6.5mm 1.00 ct	8.5x5mm 1.50 ct	8.5 x 6.5mm 1.50 ct	
8mm 2.00 ct	10x6mm 3 ct	9 x7mm 2.00 ct	
10mm 3 ct	11x9mm 5 ct	10 x 8mm 3 ct	

Here are approximate weights of round, emerald-cut, and oval diamonds in a variety of sizes. For comparison, a U.S. copper penny weighs about 12.5 carats, a nickel 25 carats, a dime 11.45 carats, and a quarter 28 carats.

About Fred Ward
and his Gem Book Series

Glamour, intrigue, romance, the quest for treasure—these are all vital aspects of humankind's eternal search and love for gemstones. For as long as people have roamed the world, they have placed extraordinary value on these incredible crystals.

Diamonds is one of seven in a series of gem books written and photographed by Fred Ward. Each book, *Opals, Diamonds, Rubies & Sapphires, Jade, Emeralds, Pearls,* and *Gem Care*, is part of a 19-year global search into the history, geology, lore, and sources of these priceless treasures. He personally has visited the sites and artifacts displayed here to provide the most authentic and timely information and photographs available in the field. Fred Ward's original articles on these topics first appeared in *National*

Fred Ward wearing Smithsonian's *Hope Diamond* and holding *The Spanish Inquisition Necklace*

Geographic Magazine. In addition to being a journalist, Mr. Ward is a Graduate Gemologist (GIA), the highest academic achievement in the gem trade.

Mr. Ward, a respected authority on gems and gemology, is in great demand as a speaker to professional and private groups. After years viewing the trade around the world, he formed Blue Planet Gems, Inc., to specialize in private searches for fine gems.

This book is part of the ongoing computer revolution of desktop publishing. It was designed with PageMaker 6.5 layouts on a Power Computing 225, using Photo CD and desktop scans. *Diamonds* was printed by H & D Graphics in Hialeah, Florida, using Adobe Janson typefaces.

At Victoria Falls, Zimbabwe

64